# Celebrate

## the God Who Loves!

S I M   P I C T O R I A L

## W. Harold Fuller

P H O T O G R A P H Y   B Y

## Jon Warren

Celebrate the God Who Loves!

Printed in Singapore


ISBN 0-919470-28-9
All Scripture quotations in this publication are from the
Holy Bible, New International Version. © 1973, 1978,
1984, International Bible Society.


Book and cover design:
Highgate Cross+Cathey Ltd.
Wheaton, IL., U.S.A.


SIM International Media
10 Huntingdale Blvd.
Scarborough, Ontario
Canada M1W 2S5
Phone: (416) 497-2424
FAX: (416) 497-2444


(Office addresses on page 136)

# THE REAL CELEBRATION

*P*eople expect some kind of celebration at the turn of a century. But when we thought about the centenary of SIM, we realized that the real celebration should not focus on a mission or its missionaries. The real celebration is that God so loved this world that He gave his only son, giving us the Good News of eternal life to announce to people everywhere.

That, we agreed, is the story to celebrate. For a century, God has given SIM the privilege and responsibility of telling that story. The astoundingly simple yet profound words of John 3:16 provide the basis for our celebration. It is easy to pass over this classic "memory verse" without understanding its significance. But as we set it in the context of today's world, it takes on startling meaning. In fact, it becomes a very up-to-date commentary on missions.

In this pictorial, John 3:16 provides the outline for five photographic essays which explore God's purpose for this world and the struggle of life against death. The photos will whisk you around the world to see what SIM missionaries and national colleagues see. The graphic scenes will bring you face to face with people God loves.

Photographer Jon Warren grew up in a missionary family in Asia and is sensitive to other cultures. He also has an artist's eye that captures the feeling of the moment.

For security reasons it would not be wise to identify some of the photos. Therefore to be consistent, we have not used names. However, in the Resource Section at the end, we have given country profiles for readers who wish to have more detailed information. We have also included a brief history of the missions which now make up today's SIM: Society for International Ministries.

We realize that the story of SIM is but a chapter in the record God is keeping, involving his people around the world in many agencies and through many centuries. He is the God who loves the people of this world, and who sends us forth to love them in his name. It was God's love that sent our pioneers out in the first place, and it is his love that keeps us soldiering on.

We believe that the familiar words of John 3:16 will take on new meaning for you as they become a graphic lens for viewing the world God loves.

W. Harold Fuller

God so loved the world

that he gave

his one and only Son

that whoever believes in him

shall not perish but have

eternal life

6

*John 3:16*

Lily Yee, Chinese Canadian, conceptualizes the theme verse in this way:

" I have chosen a global sphere, representing the world God loves, on a background of red silk kozo, a Japanese handmade paper, to represent eternity. In the Orient, red connotes life, and the broad expanse of red kozo with its fibers speaks to me of the abundance and vibrancy of eternal life.

" The eternal God entered into our world through his Son, the Living Word. In Jesus Christ we have eternal life, depicted by the words breaking out of the restriction of this globe into the red expanse."

(Calligraphy with pointed brush; Japanese hand-ground stick ink.)

# CELEBRATE THE GOD WHO LIVES

*S*ave me; you are my god!" cries the carpenter, holding up an idol he has just carved. The description is from the Prophet Isaiah, but the cry can be heard today around the world. Men and women have an innate desire to worship, and they worship objects of their own creation.

The need to worship came from God, who created Adam and Eve "in his likeness." That included the capacity and desire to love and worship their creator. Therefore only worship of him can satisfy.

But the fabrication of other gods to worship came from God's arch-enemy, Satan. Failing to usurp God's throne, Satan decided at least to rob God of worship. The Great Deceiver cares not what people worship—whether religious or secular—as long as they do not worship the living God "in spirit and in truth" (John 4:24). Satan knows that no other worship can reconcile humanity to God and bring the peace of forgiveness and assurance of eternal life.

The photographs in this first essay portray not only humanity's intense need to worship but also the variety of substitutes for faith in the living God. The substitutes are not only wooden idols. Like Isaiah's carpenter, some theologians today fashion their gods in their own image, shaping them to fit the whims of society rather than the authority of Scripture.

It is amazing that God still loves this corrupted creation. In fact, He loves the world so much that He has provided a new creation—a spiritual rebirth. He came in the person of the Son to provide the way back to himself. That amounted to a declaration of spiritual warfare, for it challenged Satan's subversion of mankind.

Messengers of the gospel step right into the arena of this spiritual conflict. Their purpose is not to deride or attack followers of other faiths. They know that "their struggle is not against flesh and blood, but against...the spiritual forces of evil in the heavenly realms."

The photos in this first section bring us face to face with that spiritual battle. In many different religious guises, Satan not only seeks to damn those who walk in darkness but also to overcome those who walk in light.

The section concludes with a reminder that men and women around the world have found deliverance from spiritual darkness through faith in the God who is alive. He is our God. This is the God we celebrate.

*God created the heavens and the earth and every living thing, including man and woman. When Adam and Eve sinned, God had to banish them from the Garden of Eden. In his love, however, God "has not left himself without testimony: He has shown kindness by giving you rain from heaven and crops in their seasons; he provides you with plenty of food and fills your hearts with joy"* (Acts 14:17).

*God had created Adam and Eve in his image, so that he could commune with them. However, after sin entered the world, humanity did not glorify the Creator. People had the innate need to worship, but they "exchanged the glory of the immortal God for images made to look like mortal man and birds and animals and reptiles" (Romans 1:23).*

*Spirit worshipers, carrying a fetish figure, take part in a chief's inauguration rite in West Africa.*

*A*t a market stall, dried animals, birds, and reptiles are offered as protection from evil and to assure success. In the background are wooden "dolls" thought to have power to ensure a woman's fertility.

*F*raming a range of the Himalayas, fluttering flags release the prayers imbued in them by Tibetan priests, Buddhists believe.

*H*indu pilgrims seek spiritual purification by washing in a tributary of the Ganges River. Hindus worship many gods, but the devotees are not aware that the living God loves them and has provided the assurance of eternal life.

*A* Buddha represents the state of enlightenment through which devotees hope to achieve the bliss of Nirvana and release from the cycle of reincarnation. Concepts of eastern mystic religions have infiltrated western society through the New Age movement.

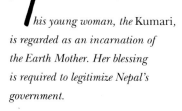

*T̲his young woman, the* Kumari, *is regarded as an incarnation of the Earth Mother. Her blessing is required to legitimize Nepal's government.*

*From Muslim mosques, five times a day the call to prayer goes out to nearly one billion followers of Islam worldwide. Their founder, Muhammad, rejected idolatry but considered Jesus to be only a prophet, not God's way of salvation as Savior and Lord.*

*Muslim worshipers demonstrate their submission (the meaning of "islam") to God by touching their foreheads to the floor or ground. However, submission can become fatalism without hope.*

*S*itting among the sandals left by devotees entering a mosque, a beggar counts his prayer beads, hoping the worshipers will give him alms as they leave. Alms-giving is among the special deeds by which Muslims try to earn salvation.

*C*amels have a proud look because only they know the one hundredth name of Allah, goes an Arab saying. Worshipers repeat the known ninety-nine names of Allah as they finger their beads—a meritorious act.

*A* Muslim student inscribes the words of Islam's Holy Koran *on his wooden "slate." Islamic learning emphasizes memorizing the* Koran *(an Arabic word from the verb, "to recite").*

*K*oranic symbols are considered sacred in themselves, and in some cases a student disciple will drink the water with which he cleans his writing palette, to obtain the spiritual benefit of the words.

*The Christianity exported to Latin America by Spanish conquistadors five hundred years ago was a morbid, fatalistic religion strongly influenced by North Africa's Islam. Christ's suffering on the cross, epitomized in these life-sized crucifixes, became an example of suffering rather than a vicarious sacrifice to be received by faith.*

*In contrast to the macabre Christ of Latin American Catholicism, the Virgin Mary is portrayed as the vibrant Queen of Heaven, the object of adoration and prayer. In a Christo-pagan melding, the indigenous people adopted her as the embodiment of their traditional Earth Mother.*

*A Peruvian Catholic devotee adds his candle to others burning in a Catholic church, hoping it will expedite his prayers to Mary and the saints, who are regarded as inter-mediaries with God.*

*A* Quechua spiritist priest offers an oblation to the Earth Mother against a backdrop of Christian crosses. Left: As he pours alcoholic beverage on an offering of burning llama meat, tongues of fire leap up— indicating acceptance by the spirits, the priest would say.

*In a relentless search for meaning to life and control of their destiny, men and women around the world try not only traditional religions but also cults and ideologies.*

*From left:*

*On African vehicles, a religious slogan is often used as a talisman to prevent accidents.*

*Gnostic churches in South America promise a new world order through knowledge.*

*In Nigeria, a cult combines Old Testament rituals with traditional spirit worship.*

*Although a discredited symbol in many lands, the hammer and sickle, here seen on a building in Asia, for some people still expresses faith in atheistic secularism to solve problems.*

*In the confusion of this pluralistic world, God has revealed himself through his Son, Jesus Christ, who declared, "I am the way, the truth, and the life. No man comes to the Father but by me." Through him many have found the eternal God. They have direct communion with him through Jesus Christ. Through his Word, the Bible, they receive spiritual nourishment and instruction in godly living. They worship the God who lives.*

so loved

# CELEBRATE A COLORFUL WORLD

*T*ravel around the world and you will come face to face with an exciting kaleidoscope of living cultures.

The colorful flags fluttering over the United Nations Assembly do not total the world's political states. There are another seventy or so that have not joined the UN, bringing the world total of nations to 223 (plus or minus a few, in our changing world). Even that figure does not reflect the number of distinct ethnic groups— over six thousand, with numerous subcultures. Even in homogenous populations, citizens are proud of their regional social cultures.

In themselves, cultures demonstrate the creativity and adaptability God has placed within the human personality. Contexts will vary, but cultures provide systems intended to help people cope with their fears and celebrate their joys. All cultures reflect human nature's fundamental drives.

However, underneath the colorful patchwork quilt of cultures, those drives, corrupted by sin, have given birth to terrifying monsters: racism, poverty, famine, disease, crime, terrorism, moral decay. Ecologists and economists alike warn of global self-destruction.

God's heart is touched by such anxiety and suffering. He sees the despair lurking beneath society's frenetic activity. He sorrows over the alienation of his creation from himself. Whatever the color, whatever the language, whatever the culture—the universal problem of sin spreads a hellish malignancy. God knew that the only antidote was to send his Son to redeem the world.

A century ago, personal concern for the world God loves led SIM pioneers to people of specific ethnic groups who did not yet know about Christ's redemption. Today SIM missionaries work in thirty-three countries, among 199 ethnic groups. Significantly, the nearly two thousand SIM missionaries themselves hail from thirty-two countries, including a number from Africa, Asia, and Latin America. They work hand in hand with indigenous churches and mission societies that are effectively incarnating the gospel in local cultures.

The gospel, they understand, transcends culture. Although history records instances of misguided destruction of culture in the name of religion (not only Christianity), that is not the purpose of the gospel of Jesus Christ. Rather, the gospel brings to the people of each culture the knowledge of the living God, and his life then purifies rather than destroys the culture. "The Bible must judge *every* culture," wrote African theologian Byang Kato.

As you view the photos in this section, celebrate with us God's love, a love that reaches out to the people of every culture.

*T*he frigid altitude of the Andes in South America influences the life style of villagers on the high plains. Many worship the Earth Mother and other spirits, thought to inhabit the mountains, such as sacred Illimani, seen here.

*F*rom one man [God] made every nation of men, that they should inhabit the whole earth; and he determined the times set for them and the exact places where they should live. God did this so that men would seek him and perhaps reach out for him and find him, though he is not far from each one of us" (Acts 17:26,27).

*I*nhabitants of Africa's Sahel have a far different life style, as they cope with the heat of semi-desert conditions. Many believe that swirling wind funnels are spirits that cause dust storms, such as this one enveloping a Somali village.

*Whatever the culture, the market place becomes a community center for buying, selling, and just getting together. This villager chooses a cola nut, either to enjoy chewing it or to give it as a token of friendship.*

*B*eneath modern and ancient
musical instruments hanging in their
market stall, Latin American girls
manufacture traditional reed flutes.

*Clutching a black doll for good luck, a Bolivian market woman displays a variety of herbal medicines. Her hat is of a type introduced by European colonialists, but now it proudly identifies her particular ethnic community.*

*With typical balancing skill, a Benin woman walks among the market people, selling freshly baked French-style bread.*

*O*n market days, this local "laundromat" in Côte d'Ivoire is extra busy. Laundrymen earn a living by washing clothes in the river. Discarded tires filled with rocks provide scrubbing platforms at just the right height.

*The gleaming towers of Abidjan on Africa's west coast are reflected in what was once a quiet fishing lagoon. The world's major cities poke through the surface of local cultures, forcing traditional life styles to adapt to the demands of a nation's development in education, industry, and world trade. But urbanization has its special problems.*

*In developing countries people pour into the cities at the worldwide rate of 160,000 a day, doubling the urban population in twenty years. The strain on services is enormous. For instance, Abidjan spends half its municipal budget on garbage disposal.*

*Highrise apartments and adobe huts fill the canyon at La Paz on Bolivia's high plains. Cities generate about two-thirds of Latin America's gross domestic product.*

*M*any who come to the cities
*seeking a better life, end up in*
*unemployment lines. For such, the*
*lure of the drug trade is powerful. In*
*some countries, drugs account for*
*greater revenue than the national*
*budget.*

*S*treet banners lend a festive air to a Pakistani city. Cities in Pakistan and India are growing at double the three percent rate considered normal. By the end of this century, over fifty percent of the world's population will live in cities.

*J*ostling for position at an intersection in a Pakistani city, a lofty camel pulling a large wagon has the advantage of being able to see over a boy riding a mule, a rickshaw operator, and a motorcyclist.

*C*hildren play outside the megacity of Manila, while in the city others earn some pocket money selling papers to passing motorists. In some countries, fifty percent of the population is under 20 years of age. Faced by poverty and broken homes, increasing numbers of children live and sleep on the streets of the world's burgeoning cities (nearly two million in Buenos Aries, two-and-a-half million in Sao Paulo).

*A* salesclerk ducks behind a mannequin as she spots our photographer through the display window of a dress shop. The Peruvian owner has purposely chosen a white model, because of the appeal of foreign fashions among educated women. International trade inevitably makes an impact on cultures—whether in the Americas or Asia, Africa or Europe.

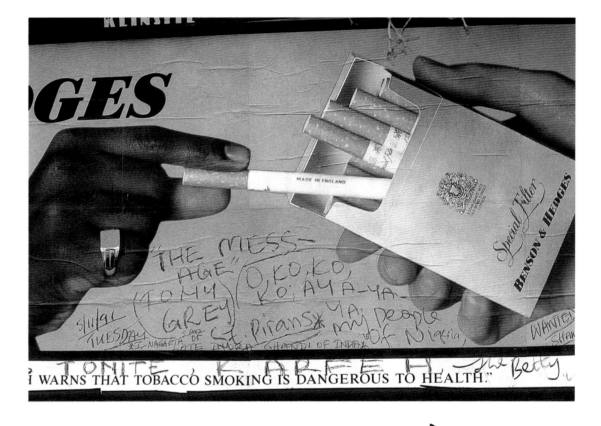

*A* tobacco advertising billboard in Africa shows a white hand offering cigarettes—appealing to the allure of international status.

*A* gasoline vendor counts the money a motorcyclist has just paid to "fill it up" with a bottle of fuel at a roadside stand. A taxi driver, unable to afford a gallon of fuel, may also purchase by the bottle—just enough for his passenger's trip.

*I*n Cotonou, Benin, motorcycle exhaust fumes fill the air as a policeman directs traffic at a city intersection. Bicycles and motorcycles are favored means of transportation in nations where a gallon of fuel may cost as much as a laborer's daily wage, and an average car may cost as much as a moderate house.

*R*eligious mores are expressed in different life styles.

*Left: Latin American Catholic teenagers socialize in mixed company at a sidewalk cafe.*

*Right: In contrast, many Asian Muslim women keep themselves completely covered while in public, and will not speak to men—even acquaintances—in public.*

*While public display of affection between men and women is the norm in some cultures, in some others men and women are strictly segregated.*

*Muslim women leaving a mosque, after worshiping separately from the men.*

*L*ooking for anything of value, a boy scuffs through burning garbage on his way back from seeking food in the city. Yet his family, squatters living in one of the cardboard-patched huts in the background, still feels better off here than facing the rigors of the parched highlands. SIM has participated with a Christian relief agency in a food program in this area.

*A*n exhausted laborer falls asleep beside a sack of produce he has carried into the city, hoping to earn enough to feed his children for a few more days. SIM ministers in some of the poorest countries in the world.

*A*lthough many rural people flee the countryside to find subsistence, all too often they find plague and death awaiting them in squalid urban quarters. A sign in a South American city warns people of the dangers of cholera, which claims thousands of lives in some parts.

*A* sorrowing mother throws herself on the casket of her child. Cultures seek to cope with death in various ways, but all humanity faces its finality.

*A*rmed soldiers patrol a city street in Peru. As if to cap the miseries faced by many urban dwellers, vice and violence add to the tensions of overgrown cities.

*M*arxist-Leninist and Maoist ideologies still prove attractive to Latin American students disillusioned by society and searching for meaning to life. Ideologues consider now-defunct European Communism as an aberration.

*T*his is the colorful, complex world God loves, in spite of its hostility to him. In fact, in his love, God "causes his sun to rise on the evil and the good, and sends rain on the righteous and the unrighteous" (Matthew 5:45).

# CELEBRATE THE GREATEST GIFT

The pilgrim painfully lifts his bleeding knees one more time, finally reaching the sacred shrine. By crawling up the hill, he hoped to merit forgiveness for his sins. Like him, followers of religions around the world struggle to earn salvation.

The gospel is unique in offering salvation freely. Through sin, God's creation had become spiritually dead. Only God could give eternal life; sinful humanity could never earn it. God so loved the world that He gave—even to the extent of sacrificing his only Son. We celebrate that greatest of all gifts.

God calls us to give ourselves fully to him. Then He sends us into the world to give ourselves so that others may know the Savior.

SIM pioneers gave themselves, sometimes to the extent of an early death. Although critics allege that missionaries go to other peoples out of cultural arrogance and adventurism, the personal journals of SIM pioneers attest to the fact that they went in the spirit of humility and servanthood. They gave themselves for the sake of those who did not know the love of the living God.

God's own giving still motivates men and women to leave their personal ambitions to serve others. They may not have to face the rigorous hardships suffered by the pioneers, but missionary service still calls for sacrificial giving.

A woman missionary may face denial of her accustomed freedoms, in order not to offend a society dominated by men and archaic taboos.

A teacher or physician may struggle without proper equipment and procedures because of shortages and work pressures.

Parents and children may choose to forego certain homeland conveniences, or to endure the stresses of frequent separations.

Supporters experience personal denial unknown by those who use their money only for themselves.

But in each instance, they give because God gave. And they give of themselves joyously, as Jesus did. He not only came into the world, but voluntarily gave himself as a ransom for it.

That divine act of giving became the pivotal point of history. The Gift himself became the Great Controversy. His own nation rejected him, and the world for which He gave his life has, for the most part, done the same. SIM knows that the gospel will be communicated effectively only as Jesus' disciples give themselves. Together we celebrate the matchless gift of the Son of God.

*I*n Peru, an SIM relief worker adds a fatherly touch to a feeding program. National Christians and missionaries give of themselves to meet the needs of a hurting world.

*A* hug of friendship, such as this boy has found at an SIM children's camp in Bolivia, may be the first introduction to God's love for many who live on the streets of cities around the world.

*S*haring the news of God's love involves respecting people's culture and participating in their daily activities—like shopping in the market or pausing for a ladle of sweet, milky tea.

*In gender-segregated cultures, it is usually easy to meet men in public—for instance, in places like this tea house.*

*However, to meet with women like this mother with her children, it takes time to build friendship.*

*P*rayer comforts a mother suffering from chronic illness, while (right) a Christian family enjoys an encouraging visit.

*A Christian woman gives her time to teach neighbors how to read, and how to respond to God's love.*

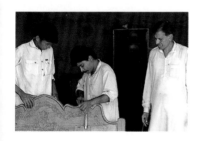

*Caring Christians give these men not only the skills to support themselves through carpentry but also the knowledge of God's supreme gift.*

*Teamwork in sharing the Good News of God's eternal gift.*

*To this missionary agronomist and his family, "giving" themselves sometimes means helping Bolivians who have relocated in a lowland area. Farmers face not only a rigorous environment but also pressures to take part in the drug trade by planting quick-growing coca. Missionaries encourage farmers to plant alternative crops to support their families.*

*I*n a program sponsored by SIM-related ECWA churches, a Nigerian veterinary assistant inoculates cattle threatened by rinderpest disease. Meeting the needs of Fulani cattleherders, national Christians and expatriate missionaries are also able to share the "Good News" with a nomadic, difficult-to-reach people.

*I*n Ethiopia, an SIM missionary shares the joy of seeing fresh water flow through a system that he and a rural development team have installed.

In some of the poorest countries in the world, church and mission teams have scooped out catchment ponds, built dams, and bored wells to bring villagers the gift of water—and the news of the one who said, "Whoever drinks the water I give him will never thirst."

81

*A*n Ethiopian mother, wearing an orthodox cross, carefully clutches her infant's medical chart as she comes to a relief clinic for help.

*T*o many facing drought and famine, basic food is a gift of love. SIM cannot turn away from emergency situations brought on by changing weather patterns, civil war, and forced migration. However, in all development programs, the Mission and its related churches encourage long-term solutions, so that suffering people do not become reliant on outside help. That may mean developing water projects, supplying hybrid seedgrains, or introducing improved strains of livestock. While maintaining its biblical priorities, SIM works closely with international aid groups to relieve suffering and develop self-reliance.

*A* family trudges home with a supply of precious food— theirs because individuals and governments around the world give generously.

*Giving, for this second-generation missionary (man with glasses), means more than hours coaching athletes at a mission school. It involves "after-hours" discipling of young lives to follow the Savior.  That is the goal of all SIM work, whether it be rugged pioneering or emergency relief work, or whether it be less spectacular ministry in classrooms, medical clinics, radio and literature offices, and other essential services. All require commitment. All involve giving.*

*A*round the world there are believers, like this Peruvian girl, who thank God that someone cared enough to bring her people the truth about God's gift of his Son.

*T*his young Bolivian is thankful that pioneer missionary George Allan gave Bolivians the Bible in their own tongue, Quechua.

87

*R*epresentative of God's people who make world missions possible, this woman, with her husband, is active not only in the local ministries of their church, but also in praying for missionaries around the world. In addition, she directs a volunteer project that collects and ships donated medical supplies to missions. She and her staff back up everything "By Prayer."

*L*ike this Asian girl, many people around the world, have the opportunity to know the living God because mission-minded Christians in other lands are praying for them. The SIM motto, "By Prayer," represents a global chain of intercession that undergirds every aspect of the work.

*I*n a creative support program, a church in a farming community in Washington State, U.S.A., sponsors "Operation Mission Harvest." Members have set aside fertile farmland to raise finances for mission projects. Volunteers plant, cultivate, harvest, and sell the grain, using the proceeds to sow the "Good Seed" worldwide. Through special projects like this or through sacrificial personal giving, God's people in many lands make it financially possible for missions to fulfill their responsibility to obey Christ's commission.

# CELEBRATE GOD'S LOVE FOR PEOPLE

What does the shoeshine urchin in Bombay have in common with the oil sheik in Kuwait—as well as the illiterate Masai cattleherder and the learned Argentine professor?

Answer: Each can receive God's salvation on exactly the same terms. Eternal life is not only for everyone, but anybody. No distinction of caste, no privilege, no bar of color, creed, or gender. Whoever—that is really something to celebrate!

This incomparable gift is available not only to the rich but also to the poor. Not just to the powerless but also to the powerful. But all must come with the simple faith of a child.

The people you will meet in this next section all started life as innocent infants. Each has been shaped by family, culture, religion, sex, race, politics, ignorance or learning. Created in God's image, nevertheless, like everyone in this world, each has been spiritually crippled by sin. A few have found spiritual life.

There was a day, we are told by the chronicler Moses, when God looked upon the world He had created and "saw how great man's wickedness on the earth had become." God was grieved, and in his holiness and righteousness He had to judge mankind.

Judgment of sin still hangs over the world, but the good news is that anyone and everyone can repent and accept God's gifts of forgiveness and eternal life.

The world's "whoevers" need someone who cares, to introduce them to the Savior, to explain the way of salvation, to love them into the family of God. SIM missionaries, themselves individuals from around the world, sinners who have found the Savior, are doing just that.

In the open market. In the restricted harem. In the classroom. In the shepherd's hut. In the highrise apartment. Meeting the children, women, and men around them. Listening, communicating. Building friendships. Sharing their faith. Teaching the Scriptures. Leading "whomever" to the Savior.

Look into the faces on these pages. Each person has a story, a joy, a hurt, a need—and a destiny. Each has made a decision about worshiping a god, but few have heard about the living God and his love for them. Some have never heard who Jesus is.

Celebrate with us the beautiful people whom God has made. Sorrow that "all have sinned and fall short of the glory of God." Rejoice that "everyone who calls on the name of the Lord will be saved." Then ask, "Lord, could I help someone like these to know you?"

*Each person on this earth is unique and special. God deals with each one personally and impartially. "God does not show favoritism" (Acts 10:34).*

*His love encompasses everyone, from the newborn infant to the aged, from the illiterate to the sophisticate.*

1. Innocent baby

2. Mischievous boy

3. Carefree girl

7. College student

8. Socialite

9. Desert nomad

4. *Farmer's daughter*

5. *Demure teen*

6. *Toiling laborer*

10. *Market vendor*

11. *Rugged warrior*

12. *Elderly businessman*

"*Everyone who calls on the name of the Lord will be saved*" (Romans 10:13).

shall not perish but

# CELEBRATE LIFE FOREVER

*G*uards shoved the male nurse into the filthy prison enclosure. "You haven't broken the law, but you are a Christian, and Christians are counter-revolutionaries!" they explained. They did assign him first aid medical duties, however.

A few weeks later the Director of Prisons enquired why behavior in that prison was so different. He discovered that the Christian nurse was conducting daily Bible study with his fellow prisoners, and even hardened criminals had become Christians. Faced with the radical change in prison behavior, the governor gave the nurse the freedom of a staff member, and eventual release.

Simply put, what happened was that the life of Christ brimmed over in one of his disciples. That is not an isolated case. Whether in repressive, totalitarian states or in open but hostile societies, committed followers of Jesus Christ demonstrate the power of the gospel. The eternal life mentioned in John 3:16 is irrepressible—like a fragrant flower blossoming on a refuse dump, so contrary to its environment yet so unassailable in its demonstration of vibrant life. Although believers still live in a world afflicted with sin's syndrome, they possess a supernatural life, here and now.

In this last photo essay you will see men, women, and children who have responded to God's love, who have found eternal life, and who want to share that life with their world. Because they know the God who loves the world, they, too, love that world in its need. They want perishing humanity around them to find life, eternal life.

They know that the alternative to eternal life is eternal death. That is a solemn thought. In Christ's name they help relieve hunger or illness or ignorance, but they are ever conscious that the paramount need of men, women, and children is to be in a saving relationship with God— to pass from darkness to light, from death to life.

To be effective in pointing others to the Savior, Jesus' disciples penetrate their multicultural world, finding ways to relate to people, to minister to their needs, to introduce them to the God who loves, and to help them grow spiritually. They are not there to debate religion or to offer alternative rituals and philosophies. Their prayer is that people will see Jesus Christ in their lives—that they will be attracted to the Savior. After all, to know him is to know life eternal. Indigenous churches around the world today demonstrate that life in their own culture.

SIM missionaries, their national colleagues, and those who enable them to minister, celebrate the life of the eternal Son of God.

*The smile reflects the internal joy of a Filipina who has found new life in Christ.*

*The word "voodoo" comes from the Fon language in Benin, West Africa. These traditional drums, instead of being used in drunken orgies of the old life, now accompany hymns of praise to God for new life in Christ.*

*An evangelistic team sings the gospel during a visit to a Fon village. Christ's followers all over the world praise God for the life that their Savior has given them. They cannot help witnessing about it, for although it is eternal, they experience it right here and now.*

*T*hose who witness often have to overcome misconceptions about Christianity and hostility to the gospel.

*T*elling others is not always easy. People like these Latin American businessmen and women may feel they are too busy to listen.

*I*n Côte d'Ivoire, a church planter shares God's Word with young men in the city. Jesus told his disciples, "You will be my witnesses... to the ends of the earth."

*T*here are walls of resistance to overcome, but this evangelist, once a Muslim himself, testifies to his people about the spiritual transformation which the life of Christ brings.

*A* second generation missionary tells people like this desert nomad about the water of eternal life.

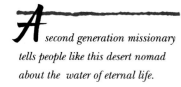

*S*haring the gospel through a reading class in Asia.

*E*ven in restrictive communities, the church of Jesus Christ is being planted. Congregations may be small, but they are vibrant.

*I*n a Muslim community in Africa, local Christians and their missionary friends worship the living Lord Jesus in a culturally relevant manner.

103

*In contrast to tiny groups of Christians meeting in countries resistant to the gospel, every Sunday this Nigerian congregation overflows its church building, with many other worshipers outside listening through open doors and windows. They are adherents of the Evangelical Churches of West Africa, outgrowth of SIM ministries, and now a fearless voice for the Christian faith. At times, government officials ask ECWA leaders for advice on national issues.*

*The president of ECWA's Women's Fellowship wears the association's official dress. Numerically strong enough to be able to have their own cloth printed, they give generously to support many of ECWA's 831 Evangelical Missionary Society workers. The women are concerned that there are still at least twenty-five million Nigerians who have never heard the gospel—many in resistant communities where EMS missionaries face strong opposition.*

*E*ducated Latin Americans in the cities traditionally have been resistant to the gospel, gripped by a ritualistic but spiritually lifeless "churchianity." Faced with major economic and social changes, many have turned to materialism. However, when presented with the biblical reality of the Christian life, men and women, like these in an urban UCE church, are finding the living Savior.

*A* Bolivian elder teaches a group of youth about the new life in Christ. Outgrowth of the pioneer work of George and Mary Allan, the Evangelical Christian Union (UCE) initially found great response in rural areas but is also developing in the cities.

*Through Christian youth groups like AWANA, boys and girls learn biblical truths that give them values for life.*

*With a wall mural of John 3:16 in the background, UCE Sunday school members take part in a children's program.*

*In Latin America, a vernacular-trained evangelist explains the Scriptures to a villager.*

*In francophone West Africa, church leaders and missionaries confer on plans for leadership training.*

*Vital to the growth of SIM-related churches in all lands of ministry is personal discipling and leadership training through Bible study. Different teaching models are used to meet different needs, from Theological Education by Extension (TEE) to graduate studies in seminary.*

*T*hese Asian young men intently study the Scriptures to prepare for Christian leadership.

*A* seminary teacher and Nigerian students enjoy a break from classes with some lively chorus singing.

*D*uring the recent Marxist-Leninist era in Ethiopia, church leaders in training often had to study in secret at night. Now they are openly studying the Bible and leading a church which survived seventeen years of oppression and persecution. SIM-related Kale Heywet churches now have 1.5 million baptized members and are active in evangelizing unreached areas.

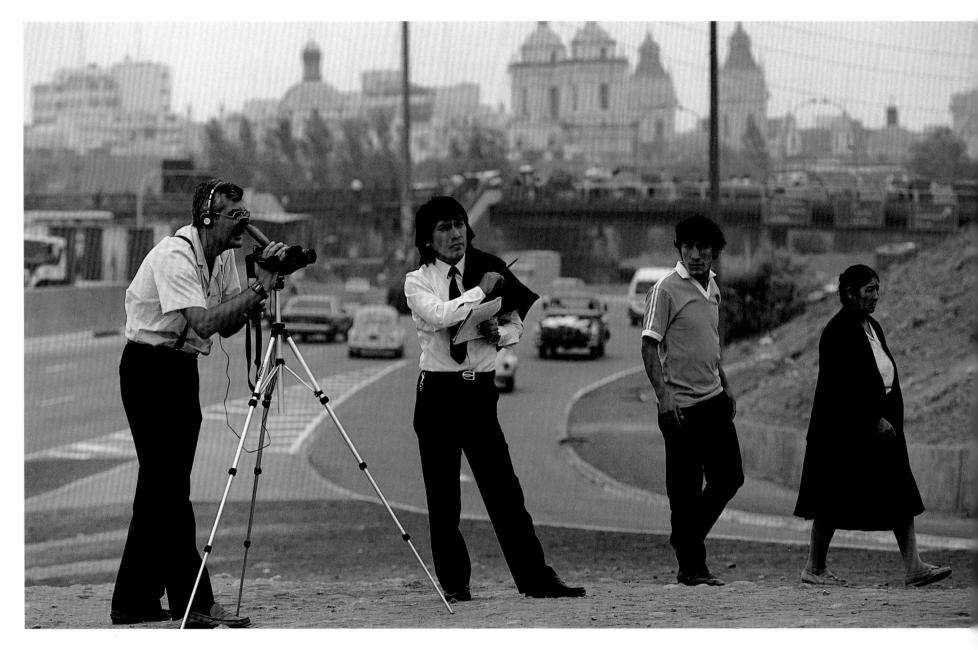

*Hard-bitten businessmen as well as questioning young people are among the viewers who watch the grass-roots program and become interested in attending a community rally or a local church service.*

*A church-planting SIM missionary (L), himself a Peruvian, uses a contemporary medium to communicate the gospel to the people of Lima, one-third of the nation's population. Obtaining a television transmitting licence, the missionary airs programs that can be viewed within a three-to-five-mile radius. An aerial can increase that to twenty miles. Moving his pocket-sized transmitter to different parts of the city, he uses the programs to interest viewers in attending local evangelistic meetings.*

*I*n the SIM recording studio in Abidjan, an SIM radio programmer directs production, recorded by his staff engineer. Tape production also has great potential, for most city dwellers are within hearing distance of the ubiquitous tape player, even if they don't have their own.

*E*ditorial staff at the French-language Evangelical Publication Center (CPE) work on the next issue of the youth magazine, Tam-Tam. SIM helped found the inter-mission publishing house, based in Côte d'Ivoire and serving all of French-speaking Africa.

*I*nto several restrictive countries in Africa and Asia, SIM beams the gospel or assists in producing programs for listeners. The Mission is also part of the World By 2000 consortium, which has the goal of making it possible, by the year 2000, for everyone to hear the gospel by radio in a language he or she understands. Several other Christian agencies which specialize in recordings are providing smaller language groups with the gospel on tape or microchip.

*I*n Benin, women return from market to their huts on stilts. SIM and its related churches in Benin broadcast to the Fon and Bariba people, assisted financially by Christian radio organizations.

*A*frican youth sit by their "boom box" as they rest in the shade of a market stall. Founded in 1954, SIM Radio ELWA broadcast the good news of eternal life in as many as 45 languages from its base in Liberia, West Africa, until the civil war in 1990. Since then, ELWA has decentralized its transmissions, using government as well as private facilities—including a restored site in Liberia.

*T*he world's mission fields, once thought of as only "over there," are found in every nation on earth. Western society is itself a vast mission field as secularism and religious pluralism have eroded Christian values. Immigrant populations are often shocked by the corrupt morals of countries they had thought of as "Christian." Evangelicals have an unparalleled opportunity to demonstrate the salvation of Jesus Christ, right in their own society.

In a London, England, suburb, a Sikh walks past a dress shop window, in which the mannequins display Indian and Pakistani styles.

*I*n London, signs like this are a reminder that we live in a post-Christian era, in which followers of Christ will be assailed not only by other religions but also by hostile secularism. Although secularists and liberal theologians join in condemning Christian missionary activity, evangelicals make no apology for defending their faith and communicating it worldwide. Christ has commanded us to do that, and He will enable us to do so, not in a spirit of arrogance and hostility, but in humility and love.

*A* double-decker bus passes a Hindu temple in a London suburb where SIM missionaries minister to ethnic minorities. Many new immigrants need a friend, and all need the Word of God. In several countries, SIM has an "Ethnic Focus" program to develop the outreach of churches to ethnic groups around them.

"**G**od so loved the world that he gave his one and only Son, that whoever believes in him shall not perish but have eternal life."

This is the world for which God gave his Son to die. This is the world to which God offers eternal life. The people of this world are a vast multitude, yes, but they are also in-dividual men and women and girls and boys, each with an immortal soul, each needing the Savior.

In its New Century, SIM recommits itself to play its part in giving the people of this world the opportunity to know God's love and receive his eternal life.

"I will praise you, O Lord, among the nations; I will sing of you among the peoples.
"For great is your love, reaching to the heavens; your faith-fulness reaches to the skies."
—Psalm 57:9,10

# A CENTENNIAL SCENARIO

*I*t seems an unlikely scenario for the formation of a mission. Unknown to each other, an evangelist sails from Australia for India, a Scottish businessman heads off to Ceylon (now Sri Lanka), a newlywed couple leave New Zealand for South America, and three youthful North Americans land in West Africa.

All of these forays take place in the same decade, three in the same year. Not only are the lead players from different countries but also from different church backgrounds. Yet one hundred years later their successors find themselves working together in one mission society.

An unlikely scenario, perhaps, but this is the remarkable story of SIM beginnings. What motivated these pioneers? How did they decide where to serve? What was happening in the 1890s to give rise to a number of missionary movements? And what eventually brought four missions together to form today's SIM?

## 1893 WAS YEAR ONE

Australian evangelist Charles Reeve left his pastoral island of Tasmania for India's crowded villages, convicted by Scripture of his obligation to share the gospel with those who had not heard. A visiting Eurasian Christian had told him about Poona (Pune), a major transit center for Hindu pilgrims and a potential base for evangelizing countless villages. In 1893, he and M. E. Gavin formed the *Poona and Indian Village Mission (PIVM)*.

In the same year, Benjamin Davidson, the Scottish businessman, formed the *Ceylon and India General Mission* (CIGM). On an earlier visit to Ceylon as agent for a pearl-trading company, he had seen the spiritual and physical plight of the people. Back in Britain, he was challenged by a visiting Sri Lankan evangelist, Tamil David, to help evangelize his people. On November 3, 1893, the Sri Lankan, having returned home, welcomed Davidson and eleven companions to his island, and within a year CIGM had opened two bases in Sri Lanka and three in India. In 1968 PIVM and CIGM merged under CIGM's new name, International Christian Fellowship (ICF).

On December 4, 1893, three young men (aged 20, 23 and 25) landed in Lagos, Nigeria, West Africa. American Tom Kent and Canadians Rowland Bingham and Walter Gowans were concerned for the estimated sixty to eighty million people of the vast area, then called The Soudan, across the widest part of Africa south of the Sahara. Within a year malaria took the lives of Gowans and Kent. Returning to Canada, Bingham recruited another team under the name Sudan Interior Mission (SIM). They were turned back by malaria, but in 1901 a third team landed and finally established a base inland.

It was also in 1893 that *The Neglected Continent* was published. This missionary report by an English Keswick conference team about their visit to South America, helped focus the concern of New Zealander George Allan and his fiance, Mary Stirling, on the Quechua people. After studying at Bible school, George and his new bride

*Charles Reeve (PIVM)*    *Benjamin Davidson (CIGM)*

*Walter Gowans, Tom Kent, Rowland Bingham (SIM)*

*George Allan (BIM)*

sailed for Argentina in 1899, and in 1907 formed the *Bolivian Indian Mission* (BIM). In 1965 BIM changed its name to Andes Evangelical Mission (AEM).

### GROWING TOGETHER

Each of these missions faced great opposition at times. The pioneers were hard hit by the physical rigors of that era, the oppressiveness of spiritual darkness, and often by violent opposition (e.g. in Bolivia at the time, evangelical preaching was punishable by death). But they persevered until they saw the Word of God take root and bear fruit. As their work has grown, each mission has been overwhelmed by the yet unfinished task.

That is why they have come together—to strengthen their hands and to be more effective. In Africa, SIM had grown in response to the enlarging opportunities on that continent. The Mission was not considering outreach in other parts of the world; there was plenty to do in Africa. But with the escalating costs of the 1980s, AEM in Latin America and ICF in Asia felt it was only good stewardship to join a larger group, in which to share representation and administration. They approached SIM, which agreed to the merger with AEM in 1982 and with ICF in 1989. In 1990 SIM reflected these mergers by changing its name to Society for International Ministries, while retaining the acronym SIM.

### DIFFERENT ROOTS, COMMON FIBERS

Today's SIM is an international partnership that grew from roots in different parts of the globe. Yet there were several common root fibers that helped to develop its present character.

The missionary initiatives at the end of the nineteenth century—and there were many more than those cited here—grew out of a time of spiritual revival. As in the case of the Apostle Paul, an overwhelming sense of Christ's love "compelled" men and women to witness to their own nation as well as to other nations worldwide. All must hear of God's redemptive love, they felt.

Although the founders of the missions that are now joined in SIM lived and worked in different corners of the earth, their lives were influenced by a common circle of Christian leaders such as H. Gratton Guinness, Samuel H. Kellogg, A. T. Pierson, A. B. Simpson, and J. Hudson Taylor. The pioneers shared their principles of dependence on God and obedience to Christ's commands.

Although all had roots in established denominations, the size of the task of world evangelism ruled out any sectarianism. They drew evangelical recruits from a wide spectrum of church backgrounds while insisting on adherence to scriptural fundamentals.

It was an era of increasing awareness of a world of diverse peoples. Rather than looking on in idle curiosity, evangelicals felt personal responsibility to share their faith. They purposely sought out ethnic groups which had the least knowledge of Christ's salvation. Even as the Apostle Paul used the communication routes of the Roman Empire, these nineteenth century missionaries utilized the trade routes of their day.

Some critics of missions allege that missionaries were colonial adventurers, extending the grasp of empire. SIM archives refute that stereotype, showing that the pioneers often opposed colonial policies. They considered the colonizers—soldiers, administrators, and traders alike—as being in as much spiritual need as the indigenous peoples, and actively sought their conversion too.

Although the message of spiritual redemption was their main focus, the pioneers led the way in alleviating physical suffering and helping to change conditions that spawned it. They protested mistreatment of native peoples and helped to bring about reform, planting Christian churches that have become salt and light in their nations.

## WHAT THE PIONEERS WOULD FIND TODAY

If we could assemble the pioneers to review the past century, they would be able to tell many stories of faith and courage, of tears and joy. But their "glory and joy," like the Apostle Paul's, would be in seeing redeemed men, women, and children. In lands where early converts were sometimes beaten, imprisoned, and even killed, they would now find strong indigenous churches making an impact on their nations. Of course, in certain lands they would still find tiny groups struggling against fierce opposition. But worldwide, adherents of SIM-related churches number some four million.

Our pioneers would be encouraged by the missionary vision which many of those churches have, extending the gospel into the dark corners of their own nations and to other nations. For instance, in Nigeria Bingham would meet the leaders of one of the world's largest indigenous missions, the Evangelical Missionary Society, which has arisen from the work that God used him to start, now known as the Evangelical Churches of West Africa.

Allan, Bingham, Davidson, and Reeve would also rejoice to meet SIM members from Asia, the Pacific, Latin America, and Africa, working alongside mission members from the pioneers' own countries. Now SIM members, totaling about two thousand, come from thirty-two countries.

The scenario of SIM beginnings may have seemed unlikely, but the scenario we shall all celebrate is what John of the Apocalypse previewed: a multitude "from every nation, tribe, people, and language, standing . . . in front of the Lamb." As we view the task ahead, we press on to help make up that multitude.

In anticipation, we join our voices in their anthem, "to him who loves us and has freed us from our sins by his blood, . . . to him be glory and power for ever and ever! Amen." That is celebration!

W. Harold Fuller

# COUNTRY PROFILES

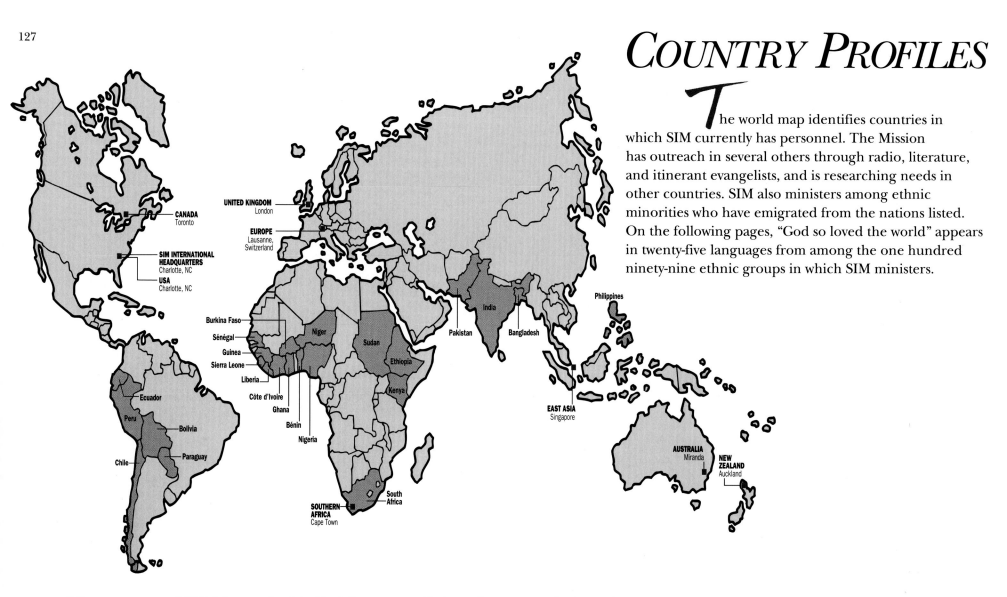

T̲he world map identifies countries in which SIM currently has personnel. The Mission has outreach in several others through radio, literature, and itinerant evangelists, and is researching needs in other countries. SIM also ministers among ethnic minorities who have emigrated from the nations listed. On the following pages, "God so loved the world" appears in twenty-five languages from among the one hundred ninety-nine ethnic groups in which SIM ministers.

CANADA
Toronto

SIM INTERNATIONAL
HEADQUARTERS
Charlotte, NC

USA
Charlotte, NC

UNITED KINGDOM
London

EUROPE
Lausanne,
Switzerland

Burkina Faso

Sénégal

Guinea

Sierra Leone

Liberia

Côte d'Ivoire

Ghana

Bénin

Nigeria

Niger

Sudan

Ethiopia

Kenya

India

Pakistan

Bangladesh

Philippines

EAST ASIA
Singapore

Ecuador

Peru

Bolivia

Chile

Paraguay

SOUTHERN
AFRICA
Cape Town

South
Africa

AUSTRALIA
Miranda

NEW
ZEALAND
Auckland

*The purpose of SIM is to glorify God by evangelizing the unreached and ministering to human need, discipling believers into churches equipped to fulfill Christ's Commission.*

# BANGLADESH

*Capital:*...............Dhaka (Dacca)

*Area:* ....................143,998 sq. km.

*Population:*...............114.8 million

*Urban population:*....................13%

*Infant mortality rate:* .......120/1000

*Literacy:*.................................29%

RELIGIONS:

*Muslim:*.............................83-87%

*Hindu:*...............................11-16%

*Buddhist:*.............................. 0.6%

*Tribal:* .....................................0.1%

*Christian:*................................0.4%

  *(Evangelical: 0.1%)*

  *Roman Catholic: 0.2%*

  *Protestant: 0.2%*

# BENIN

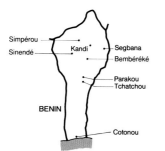

*Capitals:* ............. Porto Novo and Cotonou

*Area:* ....................112,622 sq. km.

*Population:*...................4.7 million

*Urban population:*....................39%

*Infant mortality rate:* .......110/1000

*Literacy:*.................................28%

RELIGIONS:

*Tribal religions:*........................59%

*Muslim:* ................................17%

*Christian:*................................24%

  *(Evangelical: 1.2%)*

  *Roman Catholic: 16.5%*

  *Protestant: 3.2%*

# BOLIVIA

*Capitals:*............La Paz and Sucre

*Area:* .................1,098,160 sq. km.

*Population:*...................7.3 million

*Urban population:*....................49%

*Infant mortality rate:* .......110/1000

*Literacy:*.................................75%

RELIGIONS:

*Christian:*.................................94%

  *(Evangelical: 6.5%)*

  *Roman Catholic: 83%*
  *(15% practicing)*

  *Protestant: 7.6%*

*Baha'i:* .......................................3%

# BURKINA FASO

*Capital:*...................Ouagadougou

*Area:* ....................274,200 sq. km.

*Population:*...................9.1 million

*Urban population:*......................8%

*Infant mortality:*.............126/1000

*Literacy:*..............................13.2%

RELIGIONS:

*African Traditional:*.................65%

*Muslim:* ................................25%

*Christian:*................................10%

  *(Evangelical: 1.4%)*

  *Roman Catholic: 8.5%*

  *Protestant: 1.5%*

# CAMEROON

*Capital:* ...........................Yaounde

*Area:* ....................475,442 sq. km.

*Population:*.................11.1 million

*Urban population:*....................37%

*Infant mortality rate:* .......125/1000

*Literacy:*..............................55.2%

RELIGIONS:

*African Traditional:*.................51%

*Muslim:* ................................16%

*Christian:*................................33%

  *(Evangelical: 4%)*

  *Roman Catholic: 28%*

  *Protestant: 14%*

  *Other: 12%*

Gourma

Bengali

French

Bariba

Quechua

# C E N T R A L   A F R I C A N   R E P U B L I C

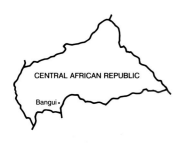

*Capital:* ...............................Bangui

*Area:* ....................622,984 sq. km.

*Population:* ...................2.9 million

*Urban population:* ...................35%

*Infant mortality rate:* .......143/1000

RELIGIONS:

*African Traditional:* .................35%

*Muslim:* ..................................15%

*Christian:* ...............................50%

   Roman Catholic: 25%

   Protestant: 25%

# C H I L E

*Capital:* ...........................Santiago

*Area:* ....................756,945 sq. km.

*Population:* .................13.2 million

*Urban population:* ...................84%

*Infant mortality rate:* ......18.5/1000

*Literacy:* ..............................94.3%

RELIGIONS:

*Christian:* .............................80.5%

   (Evangelical: 21.6%)

   Catholic: 80.7%

   Protestant: 6.1%

   Marginal groups: 2.3%

   Nonaffliated: 3.8%

*Traditional:* ............................0.8%

*Non-religious:* .......................12.8%

# C O T E   D ' I V O I R E

*Capitals:* ..........Yamoussoukro and
Abidjan

*Area:* ....................322,500 sq. km.

*Population:* .................12.6 million

*Urban population:* ...................21%

*Infant mortality rate:* .........96/1000

*Literacy:* ..............................57.3%

RELIGIONS:

*African Traditional:* ............25-40%

*Muslim:* .............................25-55%

*Christian:* ...........................20-35%

   (Evangelical: 3.7%)

   Roman Catholic: 10%

   Protestant: 4.8%

   Marginal Groups: 5.6%

# E C U A D O R

*Capital:* ...............................Quito

*Area:* ....................283,561 sq. km.

*Population:* .................10.7 million

*Urban population:* ...................54%

*Infant mortality rate:* .........63/1000

*Literacy:* ..............................69.1%

RELIGIONS:

*Christian:* .............................98.7%

   Catholic: 91-95%

   Protestant: 3.4%

   Marginal Christians: 0.8%

*Non-religious/Atheist:* .................0.7

*Traditional:* ............................0.6%

# E T H I O P I A

*Capital:* ......................Addis Ababa

*Area:* .................1,221,900 sq. km.

*Population:* .................51.7 million

*Urban population:* ...................11%

*Infant mortality rate:* ......168/1000

*Literacy:* ..................................18%

RELIGIONS:

*Christian:* ..................................57%

   (Evangelical: 9.6%)

   Ethiopian Orthodox: 41%

   Roman Catholic: 0.7%

   Protestant: 10%

*Muslim:* ..................................45%

*Tribal:* .....................................10%

*Atheist:* .....................................3%

Dieu a tant aimé le monde   French

Dios amó al mundo   Spanish

Diosca cai pachata cashnami munashcata   Quichua

Amharic

# GHANA

Capital:................................Accra
Area: ......................238,537 sq. km.
Population:....................15 million
Urban population:....................32%
Infant mortality rate: .......86/1000
Literacy:...............................53.2%

RELIGIONS:

Christian: ................................62%
   (Evangelical: 9%)
   Roman Catholic: 18.7%
   Protestant: 27.9%
   African Indigenous Groups: 16%
African Traditional: ................31%
Muslim: ..............................15.7%

Onyankopon dɔɔ wiase nie   Twi

# GUINEA

Capital:..........................Conakry
Area: ......................245,857 sq. km.
Population:...................7.3 million
Urban population:....................22%
Infant mortality rate: .......147/1000
Literacy:..............................28.3%
(The World Almanac says 48%)

RELIGIONS:

Muslim:...................................85%
African Traditional:...................5%
Christian:................................1.5%
Other: ....................................8.5%

Alla Ka dununya Kanin   Maninka

# INDIA

Capital: ........................New Delhi
Area: ................3,287,590 sq. km.
Population:...............853.4 million
Urban population:....................26%
Infant mortality rate: .........95/1000
Literacy:..................................40%

RELIGIONS:

Hindu: ...............................80.5%
Muslim: .............................11.8-13%
Christian:.............................2.61%
   (Evangelical: 0.7%)
   Roman Catholic: 1.14%
   Protestant: 1.27%
   Syrian Orthodox: 0.2%
Sikh: .....................................1.92%
Traditional: ...........................1.5%
Buddhist: ..............................0.7%
Jain: .....................................0.47%
Other: ....................................0.4%

परमेश्वर ने जगत से ऐसा प्रेम किया   Hindi

# KENYA

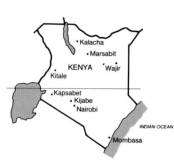

Capital: ..............................Nairobi
Area: ...................582,646 sq. km.
Population:..................24.6 million
Urban population:....................20%
Infant mortality rate: .........62/1000
Literacy:...............................59.2%

RELIGIONS:

Christian:..................................80%
   (Evangelical: 27%)
   Protestant: 29%
   Roman Catholic: 21%
   Nominal/nonaffiliated: 15%
   Marginal groups: 13%
   Orthodox: 2%
African Traditional:..............12.8%
Muslim:......................................6%
Baha'i/Hindu:.........................1.2%

Mungu aliupenda ulimwengu   Kiswahili

# LIBERIA

Capital:........................Monrovia
Area: ....................111,370 sq. km.
Population:...................2.6 million
Urban population:....................43%
Infant mortality rate: .........83/1000
Literacy:.............................18-25%

RELIGIONS:

African Traditional:............40-65%
Muslim: ...............................15-20%
Christian:.............................10-20%
   (Evangelical: 7%)
   Roman Catholic: 2%
   Protestant: 13%
   Marginal groups: 4%

(statistics pre-1991 war)

Ngala jei lɔwɔlɔi hu loi ngwala   Gbandi

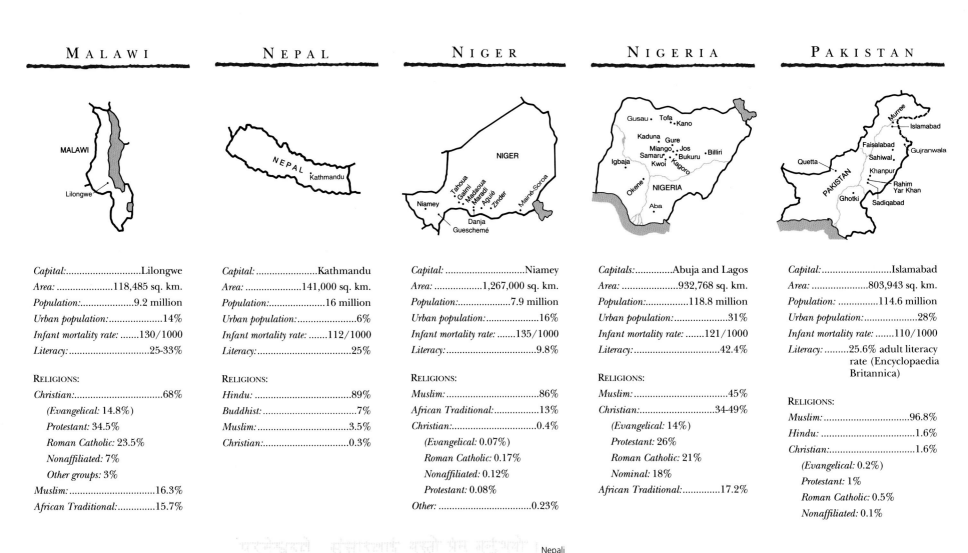

# MALAWI

Capital:.........................Lilongwe

Area:.................118,485 sq. km.

Population:...................9.2 million

Urban population:....................14%

Infant mortality rate: .......130/1000

Literacy:...............................25-33%

RELIGIONS:

Christian:.................................68%

(Evangelical: 14.8%)

Protestant: 34.5%

Roman Catholic: 23.5%

Nonaffiliated: 7%

Other groups: 3%

Muslim:...............................16.3%

African Traditional:..............15.7%

# NEPAL

Capital:......................Kathmandu

Area:.....................141,000 sq. km.

Population:...................16 million

Urban population:.....................6%

Infant mortality rate: .......112/1000

Literacy:.......................................25%

RELIGIONS:

Hindu:.......................................89%

Buddhist:......................................7%

Muslim:.....................................3.5%

Christian:...................................0.3%

# NIGER

Capital: ...........................Niamey

Area:.................1,267,000 sq. km.

Population:...................7.9 million

Urban population:....................16%

Infant mortality rate: .......135/1000

Literacy:......................................9.8%

RELIGIONS:

Muslim:.......................................86%

African Traditional:.................13%

Christian:..................................0.4%

(Evangelical: 0.07%)

Roman Catholic: 0.17%

Nonaffiliated: 0.12%

Protestant: 0.08%

Other: .....................................0.23%

# NIGERIA

Capitals:.............Abuja and Lagos

Area:.....................932,768 sq. km.

Population:...............118.8 million

Urban population:....................31%

Infant mortality rate: .......121/1000

Literacy:.....................................42.4%

RELIGIONS:

Muslim:.......................................45%

Christian:................................34-49%

(Evangelical: 14%)

Protestant: 26%

Roman Catholic: 21%

Nominal: 18%

African Traditional:..............17.2%

# PAKISTAN

Capital:..........................Islamabad

Area:.....................803,943 sq. km.

Population: ..............114.6 million

Urban population:....................28%

Infant mortality rate: .......110/1000

Literacy: .........25.6% adult literacy
rate (Encyclopaedia
Britannica)

RELIGIONS:

Muslim:...................................96.8%

Hindu: ....................................1.6%

Christian:................................1.6%

(Evangelical: 0.2%)

Protestant: 1%

Roman Catholic: 0.5%

Nonaffiliated: 0.1%

Nepali

Cheyao

Hausa

Tamajaq

Urdu

# PARAGUAY

Capital: ......................Asuncion
Area: ...................406,752 sq. km.
Population: ...................4.3 million
Urban population: ....................43%
Infant mortality rate: ........42/1000
Literacy:............................ 85%

RELIGIONS:

Christian: .............................98.4%
   (Evangelical: 2%)
   Catholic: 96% (40% practicing)
   Protestant: 2.3%
Traditional: ............................0.7%
Atheist:.................................0.6%
Marginal: ..............................0.3%

# PERU

Capital: ...................................Lima
Area: ..................1,284,640 sq. km.
Population:..................21.9 million
Urban population:....................69%
Infant mortality rate: .........76/1000
Literacy:.................................87%

RELIGIONS:

Christian:................................98%
   (Evangelical: 5%)
   Roman Catholic: 81%
   Protestant: 5%
Traditional: ...............................1%
Other: .......................................13%

# PHILIPPINES

Capital: ............................Manila
Area: ....................300,000 sq. km.
Population: .................66.1 million
Urban population:....................42%
Infant mortality rate: .........48/1000
Literacy:.................................89%

RELIGIONS:

Christian:...............................89.1%
   (Evangelical: 6.4%)
   Roman Catholic: 63.6%
   Indigenous Catholics: 8%
   Indigenous Marginals: 6.1%
   Foreign Marginals: 0.7%
   Protestant: 10.7%
Muslim:...............................6-8.4%
Non-religious:...........................1.5%
Traditional: .............................1-2%

# SENEGAL

Capital:................................Dakar
Area: ....................196,840 sq. km.
Population:....................7.4 million
Urban population:....................36%
Infant mortality rate: .......128/1000
Literacy:.................................20%

RELIGIONS:

Muslim:................................90.9%
African Traditional:................4.6%
Christian:................................4.5%
   (Evangelical: 0.09%)
   Roman Catholic: 3.5%
   Protestant: 1%

# SIERRA LEONE

Capital: ..........................Freetown
Area: ......................72,325 sq. km.
Population:....................4.2 million
Urban population:....................28%
Infant mortality rate: .......154/1000
Literacy:.................................15%

RELIGIONS:

African Traditional:................50%
Muslim:...................................40%
Christian:................................10%
   (Evangelical: 1.5%)
   Protestant: 6.1%
   Nonaffiliated: 2%
   Roman Catholic: 1.6%
   Marginal groups: 0.3%

Dios amó al mundo    Spanish

Yälla dafa bëgg àddina bi    Wolof

Sinisinta ng Dios ang sanglibutan    Tagalog

God so loved the world    English

## S O M A L I A

Capital: ......................Mogadishu
Area: ..................638,803 sq. km.
Population: ...................8.4 million
Urban population: ...................33%
Infant mortality rate: ......132/1000
Literacy: .......................................6%

RELIGIONS:
Sunni Muslim: .....................99.8%
Christian: ...............................0.1%
   (Evangelical: possibly 800)
   Roman Catholic: 2,100
   (in number, all expatriates)
   Protestant: 1,000 in number
   Other: 0.1%

## S O U T H   A F R I C A

Capitals: ......Pretoria/Cape Town
Area: ................1,221,041 sq. km.
Population: ....................39.6 million
Urban population: .................56%
Infant mortality rate: ........55/1000
Literacy: ....................................64%

RELIGIONS:
Christian: ............................77.5%
   (Evangelical: 8% est.)
   Protestant: 47.5%
   African Independent: 21%
   Roman Catholic: 10%
   Miscellaneous: 0.5%
African Traditional: ................11%
Atheist/Non-religious: .............2.5%
Hindu: .........................................2%
Muslim: ..................................1.5%
Unknown: ...............................5.5%

## S R I   L A N K A

(formerly Ceylon)
Capital: ...........................Colombo
Area: .......................65,600 sq. km.
Population: .................16.4 million
Urban population: ...................24%
Literacy: ...................................90%

RELIGIONS:
Buddhist: .................................69%
Hindu: ...................................15.4%
Muslim: ..................................7.6%
Christian: ...............................7.4%
   (Evangelical: 0.2%)
   Roman Catholic: 6.3%
   Protestant: 0.75%

## S U D A N

Capital: ............................Khartoum
Area: ..................2,505,813 sq. km.
Population: ....................25.2 million
Urban population: ......................20%
Infant mortality rate: .........108/1000
Literacy: .................................21.6%

RELIGIONS:
Muslim: ........................................73%
Christian: .................................14.9%
   (Evangelical: 1.6%)
   Roman Catholic: 5.6%
   Protestant: 3.1%
   Nominal: 0.7%
   Other: 0.8%
African Traditional: .................10.9%
Non-religious/atheist: .................1.2%

## Z A I R E

Capital: ...........................Kinshasa
Area: ................2,345,000 sq. km.
Population: .................36.6 million
Urban population: ...................40%
Infant mortality rate: ......103/1000
Literacy: ...................................45%

RELIGIONS:
Christian: ...........................88-92%
   (Evangelical: 17.6%)
   Roman Catholic: 42%
   Protestant: 28%
African Traditional: .............8-12%
Muslim: ...................................1.4%

Tamil

Somali

Arabic

Afrikaans

Koma

SIM is pleased to provide services and materials to assist schools, churches, prayer groups, and individuals in promoting the cause of world evangelization. Write the offices listed below for information about the following:

## COUNSELLING

SIM offices have candidate secretaries who can advise churches, schools, and individuals on developing a missions program, and on opportunities and procedures for serving in missions. Conference speakers are also available.

## SEMINARS

SIM has a program to help churches develop local outreach among ethnic minorities. Other seminars include understanding how to approach people of non-Christian religions, and cross-cultural awareness.

## PRAYER GROUPS

SIM puts its motto, "By Prayer," into practice in developing prayer groups and keeping them informed with up-to-date prayer information.

## CURRENT OPPORTUNITIES

SIM offices can share monthly updates of strategic opportunities for service in Africa, Asia, and South America, as well as in other areas. Each has a description of the ministry and qualification needed.

## PUBLICATIONS AND AUDIOVISUALS

The following is a selection. Your SIM office will gladly send you a complete catalog of publications and audiovisuals.

*SIMNOW:*
To keep informed of SIM ministries in Africa, South America and Asia, write for a free subscription to this 16-page magazine.

Catalog:
SIM offices will gladly send you a catalog of published materials and audiovisuals. Sample titles:

Books:
*Fire on the Mountains*
by Raymond Davis. The miraculous birth of the church in southern Ethiopia.

*The Winds of God*
by Raymond Davis. How Ethiopian evangelists reached throughout southern Ethiopia.

*Tread Upon the Lion*
by Sophie de la Haye. The story of West Africa pioneer Tommy Titcombe.

*Tie Down the Sun*
by W. Harold Fuller. A travelog about Latin America, from its indigenous peoples to its current challenge.

*Condor of the Andes*
by Peter Wagner and Joe McCullough. The story of South America's first missionary pilot.

Audiovisuals:
*The Race*
A challenging documentary of results of the spiritual race begun by three missions in the 1890s, culminating in today's SIM. 15mins.

*Power by Prayer*
A Biblical look at intercessory prayer. 26 mins. VHS video, 16mm film.

*No Unreachables*
Once-"unreachable people" who are now part of the church. 26 mins. VHS video, 16mm film.

*Talking Guidance, Talking Mission*
Personal guidance experiences. 29 mins. VHS video.

*Showing That We Care*
Meeting human need through development ministries. 29 mins. VHS video, 16mm film.

*Who Sends Them?*
The local church and missions. 23 mins. VHS video.

For Children:
*Rick-a-Chee*
series, by Edna Menzies. Six large-page illustrated stories about a small African boy.
**Also Available on Video!**

*Never Hide a Hyena in a Sack*
by Ines Penny. Biblical lessons in life from African folklore.

## A U S T R A L I A
Locked Bag 2
Taren Point Centre
NSW 2229
Australia
Tel: (61-2) 525-8355
Fax: (61-2) 526-1700

## C A N A D A
10 Huntingdale Blvd.
Scarborough, ON
Canada, M1W 2S5
Tel: (416) 497-2424
Fax: (416) 497-2444

## E A S T   A S I A
SIM East Asia
116 Lavender St.
#04-09 Pek Chuan Bldg.
Singapore 1233
Tel: (65) 298-3611
Fax: (65) 298-6751

## E U R O P E
Case Postale 42
1000 Lausanne 20
Switzerland
Tel: (41-21) 25-51-39
Fax: (41-21) 24-76-78
Attn: SIM 25-51-39

## N E W   Z E A L A N D
P.O. Box 38-588
Howick, New Zealand
Tel: (64-9) 535-4913
Fax: (64-9) 535-7961

## S O U T H E R N   A F R I C A
Private Bag XI
Clareinch 7740
RSA
Tel: (27) 21-696-1922
Fax: (27) 21-696-3205
Attn: SIM

## U N I T E D   K I N G D O M
Ullswater Crescent,
Coulsdon
Surrey  CR5 2HR
England
Tel: (44-81) 660-7778
Fax: (44-81) 763-1175

## U N I T E D   S T A T E S
Box 7900
Charlotte, NC
U.S.A.  28241-7900
Tel: (704) 588-4300
Fax: (704) 587-1518